PASSAGE TO SLAVERY, JOURNEYS TO FREEDOM

←- Transatlantic slave routes

← Selected routes of black loyalists

◄•••• Thomas Peters' journey to London

ENGLAND

London

EUROPE

ATLANTIC OCEAN

600 miles

600 kilometers

AFRICA

Beginning in the 15th century, captured Africans were shipped across the Atlantic Ocean from a number of seaports on the African coast. They were sold as slaves to colonists of the Americas. The slave trade was banned by English law in 1807, but slavery continued to be legal in the United States until 1865.

To South America

Freetown • SIERRA LEONE

LIBERIA

LIBERTY OR DEATH

LIBERTY
or DEATH

The Surprising Story of
RUNAWAY SLAVES
Who Sided with the British During the
AMERICAN REVOLUTION

BY MARGARET WHITMAN BLAIR

NATIONAL GEOGRAPHIC

WASHINGTON, D.C.

CONTENTS

—◇◇◇◇◇◇—

SLAVERY AS BUSINESS
Captured Africans were herded like animals to the coast and then shipped across the Atlantic. Those who survived the terrible journey were sold for big profits to be unpaid workers for the rest of their lives in the Americas.

FOREWORD

Liberty and freedom are not the sole province of any set of people anywhere. The fact that three of the first four Presidents of our nation were slaveholders would seem to suggest that our nation was founded in slavery.

Patrick Henry was a strong supporter of the American Revolution. As children in school, we were required to read, memorize, and recite his famous "Liberty or Death" oration. What he had to say was this: "Is life so dear, or peace so sweet, as to be purchased at the price of chains and slavery? Forbid it, Almighty God! I know not what course others may take; but as for me, give me liberty or give me death!" I was born and raised in Richmond, Virginia, eight blocks away from St. John's Church, the place where the speech was made. When I had occasion to visit there with my schoolmates, I came away puzzled and confused.

I asked my father, whose mother and father were both slaves freed after the Civil War, how we could speak of liberty and justice when the freedom Henry spoke of was the freedom to deny others their own freedom. He had no kind words to say about Henry.

Liberty or Death illustrates this glaring incongruity in our nation's beginning by following those slaves who chose to join the British cause, fighting for their own freedom and against the revolting colonies. It allows readers to

THE FIGHT FOR FREEDOM

Crispus Attucks (shown being shot above) was one of five people killed during the Boston Massacre at the beginning of the American Revolution. He is one of countless African Americans who made significant contributions to American history.

—〰〰〰—

come to appreciate our efforts to correct and make right our views of freedom as they pertain to individuals of any class, color, or religion.

America has gone through its "dark age"; let the age of enlightenment continue.

L. Douglas Wilder
Former and first black governor of Virginia

LIBERTY

"AND I DO HEREBY FURTHER DECLARE ALL INDENTURED SERVANTS, NEGROES, OR OTHERS, (APPERTAINING TO REBELS,) FREE THAT ARE ABLE AND WILLING TO BEAR ARMS, THEY JOINING HIS MAJESTY'S TROOPS AS SOON AS MAY BE . . . TILL SUCH TIME AS PEACE MAY BE AGAIN RESTORED TO THIS AT PRESENT MOST UNHAPPY COUNTRY. . ."

— LORD DUNMORE, 1775

Chapter 1

to SLAVES

SPRING 1775

he blossoms bloomed as usual in the first warm days of spring, yet there was a chill in Virginia's capital of Williamsburg. The Royal Governor, Lord Dunmore, had shut down the Virginia House of Burgesses, the colony's elected assembly. Dunmore was angry because they had declared a day of fasting and prayer for the people of Boston, who were being punished because a small group of radicals had dumped imported British tea into their harbor to protest taxes. The Burgesses defied the Governor's ban by leaving town to meet at a church in Richmond. At that meeting, they approved the creation of armed militias, and they elected their representatives to a Continental Congress that would consider what should be done about Britain's treatment of its colonies in America. One of those chosen to attend was Patrick Henry, who brought the men to their feet with his fiery words: "Give me liberty or give me death!" Revolution was brewing in Virginia.

Late one night, Lord Dunmore ordered a small group of royal marines to remove the colony's store of gunpowder from the powder house in Williamsburg and to load it onto a British warship. When the theft was discovered, an angry crowd gathered to confront the governor. To allay the people's fury, Lord Dunmore claimed he'd heard that some slaves were planning an uprising and he'd worried they might try to seize the gunpowder. Many of those gathered did not believe him—although with Williamsburg's 52 percent black population, they were aware that an uprising was a potential threat. What they really suspected was that Dunmore feared rebellious Virginians would use the gunpowder against him.

Messengers on horseback spread the news in the countryside that the governor had stolen the gunpowder. Would he take away their weapons next? Further arousing them was news of a battle between British soldiers and colonial militias at the towns of Lexington and Concord, Massachussetts, where blood had spilled on both sides. Soon, militias made up of hundreds of armed men, including a group led by Patrick Henry, began marching toward Williamsburg, with the aim of forcing the governor to return their gunpowder.

Greatly outnumbered, Dunmore made a dramatic threat. After placing cannons around his residence and arming his servants, he sent word to the men marching ever closer toward him:

"By the living God, if any insult is offered to me, or to those who have obeyed my orders, I will declare freedom to the slaves and reduce the city of Williamsburg to ashes!"

Lord Dunmore talked of freeing the slaves? Living in luxury in the Governor's Palace, he owned 56 slaves and employed a dozen servants. But he knew such a threat would strike terror into Virginians.

The wealthier southern colonists depended on slave labor to work their large fields, and slavery was legal in all thirteen colonies. These workers originally came from Africa, where they were captured, sold into slavery, transported across the Atlantic Ocean in chains, and then forced to work long hours without pay. Once sold, they belonged to the master, and any children they bore became the master's property, too. As the number of

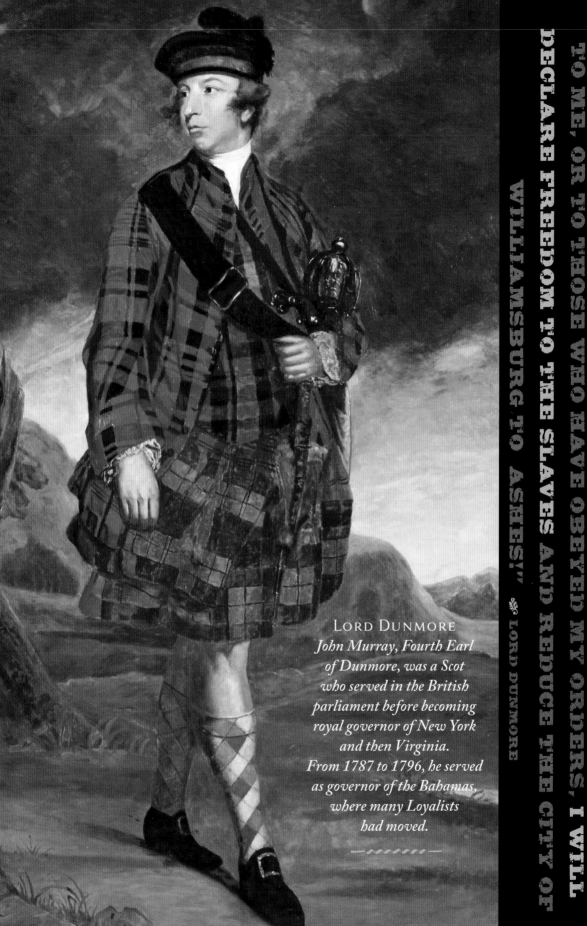

"BY THE LIVING GOD, IF ANY INSULT IS OFFERED TO ME, OR TO THOSE WHO HAVE OBEYED MY ORDERS, I WILL DECLARE FREEDOM TO THE SLAVES AND REDUCE THE CITY OF WILLIAMSBURG TO ASHES!" ❧ LORD DUNMORE

LORD DUNMORE
*John Murray, Fourth Earl
of Dunmore, was a Scot
who served in the British
parliament before becoming
royal governor of New York
and then Virginia.
From 1787 to 1796, he served
as governor of the Bahamas,
where many Loyalists
had moved.*

A LIFE OF ENDLESS TOIL
Slaves pick cotton in the field of a plantation.

slaves grew, white colonists feared they might organize and try to overthrow their masters by force.

By threatening to free the slaves, Dunmore played on this deep-seated fear. He also realized that if there were an American rebellion, it would take months to get troops from England. If he recruited slaves, he could quickly swell his small band of marines.

Freeing slaves would also make life hard for the rebels. Leaders like George Washington, Patrick Henry, and Thomas Jefferson relied on the work of many slaves to run their plantations. Lord Dunmore hoped that if their slaves ran away, rebellious land owners would not have the time or resources to wage war.

Dunmore did not need to carry out his immediate threat, for a representative of the governor and Patrick Henry reached a compromise. The governor paid the colonists for the gunpowder he had seized.

But throughout the colonies the revolutionary spark had been struck.

Militias continued to drill and to train. New Englanders captured Fort Ticonderoga, gaining cannon and a large supply of gunpowder. As the Continental Congress met in Philadelphia to debate on whether to separate from Britain, by force if necessary, they watched two thousand citizen soldiers march past.

Back in Virginia's capital, a nervous Dunmore decided it was time to leave town. Taking his wife and children, he slipped out in the middle of the night onto a waiting British warship. Then he sent his family back to England, while he stayed on the warship. With him were his band of royal marines and the slaves he had lured with a promise of freedom. His ranks were also swelled by some British troops stationed in St. Augustine, Florida, who had sailed north to join him.

—~~~~~~—

THE ESCAPE

British troops in a rowboat near the English man-of-war ship Fowey *where Lord Dunmore lived after he fled the Governor's Palace in Williamsburg*

"IF A GOVERNOR CAN. . .
GIVE FREEDOM
TO OUR... SLAVES,
LET US BID ADIEUS
TO EVERY THING VALUABLE
IN LIFE."

EDMUND PENDLETON, PRESIDENT OF GENERAL
CONVENTION, DECEMBER 13, 1775

Dunmore's flotilla of ships raided rebels' riverside plantations. During these surprise attacks, they took fresh water, food, and weapons. They also picked up any slaves willing to join them. Local slaves knew the waterways better than Dunmore's men and were skilled at piloting the small boats used on such raids.

Dunmore's men used Norfolk, a town four times larger than Williamsburg, as a land base. Living there was a group of Scottish merchants who traded with England and wanted to stay part of the British Empire. Many loyalists (also called Tories after the dominant political party in England) moved to England to avoid the war, but others joined Dunmore's "floating town." Many of those who stayed signed an oath of loyalty to the Crown.

ETHIOPIAN REGIMENT

Loyalist John Singleton Copley painted the 1781 death of Major Francis Pierson at the Battle of Jersey in the Channel Islands (between England and France). Copley included a black soldier in the Royal Ethiopian uniform in his painting, even though the unit could not possibly have fought there.

WHEN DUNMORE learned that 300 rebels planned to march on his stronghold at Norfolk, he decided to strike first. Dunmore's force of 100 surprised the colonists at a place on the Elizabeth River called Kemp's Landing on November 14, 1775. Former slaves captured one of two enemy commanding officers. Other Virginia militia were killed, wounded, or captured, and the rest fled. Contrary to popular expectations, freed slaves had fought well, and their fearless efforts inspired Dunmore to try to attract more to his side.

He organized the men into two regiments: one for the white loyalists called The Queen's Own Loyal Regiment and one for the blacks known as Lord Dunmore's Ethiopian Regiment. In those days, *Ethiopian* was a broad label meaning "Black."

Before the battle at Kemp's Landing, Dunmore, angered by a nasty article about him, had sent a landing party from his ship to arrest the publisher of a Norfolk newspaper. The publisher escaped, but soldiers seized his printing press. After his victory at Kemp's Landing, Dunmore used the captured printing press to finally follow through on his threat. He printed a proclamation offering freedom to slaves who fought on the side of the king. This offer was only for slaves whose masters were in rebellion, however, because he didn't want to anger loyalist Virginian slave owners.

The proclamation was picked up and reprinted in the newspapers, and it provoked many furious responses from slave owners. One wrote a letter to the editor warning that if the British were to win, the patriots' lands would be taken and "our negroes will be sold as part of our estates, probably in the West Indies, where their condition will be ten times worse than it is now." The writer also noted of Lord Dunmore himself that "till his scheme of calling on them for assistance, he was cruel to his own [slaves], and was frequently heard to wish that there was not one negro in the country." The letter writer warned that if slaves were caught trying to run away to Lord Dunmore, they would be hanged, and their wives and children would be punished. The letter then ended with the assertion that slaves should be "contented with their situation and expect a better condition in the next world, and not run a risk of being unhappy here and miserable hereafter."

—⁓⁓⁓—

LORD DUNMORE'S PROCLAMATION
Although Lord Dunmore did it for strategic reasons rather than to help the enslaved, his proclamation to free the slaves who fought for the British was the first emancipation proclamation, long before President Lincoln's during the American Civil War.

Iis Excellency the Right Honorable JOHN Earl of DUNMORE, His
ajesty's Lieutenant and Governor General of the Colony and Dominion of
rginia, and Vice Admiral of the fame.

PROCLAMATION.

I have ever entertained Hopes, that an Accommodation might have
taken Place between GREAT-BRITAIN and this Colony, without being
elled by my Duty to this moft difagreeable but now abfolutely neceffary
rendered fo by a Body of armed Men unlawfully affembled, firing on His
sty's Tenders, and the formation of an Army, and that Army now on
March to attack His MAJESTY's Troops and deftroy the well difpofed Sub-
of this Colony. To defeat fuch treafonable Purpofes, and that all fuch
rs, and their Abettors, may be brought to Juftice, and that the Peace, and
Order of this Colony may be again reftored, which the ordinary Courfe
Civil Law is unable to effect; I have thought fit to iffue this my Pro-
ion, hereby declaring, that until the aforefaid good Purpofes can be ob-
I do in Virtue of the Power and Authority to ME given, by His MAJE-
letermine to execute Martial Law, and caufe the fame to be executed
hout this Colony: and to the end that Peace and good Order may the
be reftored, I do require every Perfon capable of bearing Arms, to refort
MAJESTY's STANDARD, or be looked upon as Traitors to His
ry's Crown and Government, and thereby become liable to the Penalty
w inflicts upon fuch Offences; fuch as forfeiture of Life, confifcation of
&c. &c. And I do hereby further declare all indented Servants, Negroes,
rs, (appertaining to Rebels,) free that are able and willing to bear Arms,
oining His MAJESTY's Troops as foon as may be, for the more fpeedily
g this Colony to a proper Senfe of their Duty, to His MAJESTY's
and Dignity. I do further order, and require, all His MAJESTY's Leige

Many slaves discounted such warnings. They believed Dunmore's promise to emancipate them. Moreover, slaves were likely inspired by all the talk of freedom in the air. Household servants heard their masters decry the British government's attempt to "enslave" the colonists. There were excited discussions about all people having "natural rights," including the "inalienable" right to be free. Of course, when men said all people had the right to be free, they did not mean to include their black slaves, or even their wives. But all that heady talk of freedom! Word of Dunmore's Proclamation with his offer to free the slaves spread like wildfire among plantations.

Dunmore sent couriers and spies all over Virginia to distribute and publicize his proclamation. He ordered crews out on small boats to invite any slaves they met to come on board and join them. Two weeks later, 300 runaway slaves had signed up. Slave-owning patriots became nervous. In coastal areas, night-time patrols were stepped up, and roads out of town were watched. Meanwhile, more and more slaves fled to Dunmore's ships, a total of about 800 by early 1776.

Somerset DECISION

Even before Lord Dunmore's emancipation proclamation, word had spread among the slaves that they could become free if they could escape to England. This was largely because of a famous court case decided in London in 1772. In the Somerset Decision (named for the slave defendant named James Somerset), a British judge ruled that a slave could not be forcibly removed from English soil and imprisoned on a ship bound for a British colony where slavery was legal (in this particular case, Jamaica). Many people interpreted this to mean that slavery was illegal in England.

DELIVERING THE NEWS

This 1977 painting by Vernon Wooten shows a British soldier reading the Dunmore Proclamation to an African-American slave. Many slaves were not allowed to learn to read and therefore probably could not have read the proclamation for themselves.

IN HIS PROCLAMATION, Dunmore had tried to recruit able-bodied men who could fight in exchange for liberty, but young girls and women fled to him, too. Some women escaped with their husbands. Others came alone or with children, swelling the number of Dunmore's followers. Desperate for freedom, the ones without boats swam or dog-paddled out to the ships. Those caught and returned to their masters were punished. They could be hanged or confined to jail, and later some were sent to work in the lead mines.

Lord Dunmore had a hard time providing for and making use of all the runaways. Those he organized into his Ethiopian Regiment had no experience with military discipline, weapons, or battles. His officers had to train them quickly—a problem the Patriots were facing with their white soldiers as well.

The former slaves' passion for freedom would have to compensate for their lack of military experience. To remind them and inspire them, the motto "Liberty to Slaves" was embroidered on their uniforms' shirts.

AND SOME JOINED

"WHY STAND WE HERE **IDLE**? WHAT IS IT THAT GENTLEMEN **WISH**? WHAT WOULD THEY HAVE? IS **LIFE** SO DEAR, OR PEACE SO SWEET, AS TO BE **PURCHASED** AT THE PRICE OF CHAINS AND SLAVERY? **FORBID** IT, ALMIGHTY GOD! I KNOW NOT WHAT COURSE OTHERS MAY TAKE; BUT AS FOR ME, GIVE ME **LIBERTY** OR GIVE ME **DEATH!**"

— PATRICK HENRY, 1775

the PATRIOTS

APRIL 1775

atriots who wanted independence from England, as well as the rights to make their own laws and to levy their own taxes, were ready to lay down their lives if necessary. But the rights they were willing to fight for were to be only for landowning gentlemen like themselves. So the inscription on the chests of Dunmore's Ethiopian Regiment was a pointed rejoinder to Patrick Henry's dramatic declaration: "liberty or death." Liberty for whom? Slaves wanted liberty, too!

At the beginning, the American side was reluctant to have blacks fighting. Some of the men most active in the independence movement—George Washington, Thomas Jefferson, and Patrick Henry, to name just a few—were wealthy plantation-owning southerners, which meant they owned many slaves. They thought it dangerous to arm black men, and they were also uncomfortable with the idea of having black men fight for the freedom of others without letting them have their own freedom. Others among the Patriots, such as Washington's French ally General Lafayette, had no hesitation in embracing blacks in the military, even from the outset.

"NEITHER THE HUE OF THEIR COMPLEXION NOR THE BLOOD OF AFRICK HAVE ANY CONNECTION WITH COWARDICE."

NEW JERSEY OFFICIAL ADVANCING PLAN TO ALLOW BLACKS IN MILITARY, AUGUST 1776

AMERICAN
SOLDIERS
*This old drawing
shows an African–
American soldier (left)
in the uniform of the
First Rhode Island
Regiment, the first
nearly all-black unit
in American
military history.*

After Dunmore's Proclamation, and the initial horror at arming slaves or even former slaves wore off, especially in the North, there were second thoughts about the wisdom of excluding blacks. As time went on, the American side became desperate for fighting men of whatever color. Some states, such as Connecticut and Vermont, ruled that if a master permitted it, he could free you in order to fight. In others, such as Massachusetts and Rhode Island, free blacks could serve; or the state could buy and emancipate slaves willing to become soldiers. It is thought that about 5,000 blacks served with the American troops. While it is a far smaller number than those who escaped to British protection (estimated to be closer to 15,000 or 20,000, though some put the number closer to 80,000 or 100,000), they were still a considerable source of strength. It is hard to know the precise number because most of the American units were integrated, and the race of those who enlisted usually was not recorded.

Many of the black men who fought against the British performed with valor at the early battles, fighting side by side with white patriots. A slave from Lexington, Massachusetts, named Prince Easterbrooks, was one of the first to take a bullet at Concord Bridge; he survived and went on to fight in

Crispus ATTUCKS

In a sense, the very first casualty of the American Revolution was a former slave living in Boston. Crispus Attucks—believed to have been of mixed race with an African father and a Natick Indian mother—had likely run away to be free and then found work as a sailor. A tall and imposing man, Attucks led a group of Bostonians who joined children throwing snowballs at British soldiers on guard duty. Attucks and his men brandished heavy sticks at the soldiers on that infamous evening of March 5, 1770. The nervous soldiers fired their rifles into the crowd. First to fall, with two bullets to the chest, was Crispus Attucks. Two others died immediately, and two shortly afterward. Known ever after as the Boston Massacre, the event would become a rallying cry for American patriots. It is interesting to note that lawyer John Adams, later to become a revolutionary leader and later the second President of the United States, successfully defended the British soldiers against murder charges.

nearly every major campaign of the war. Peter Salem, a slave in Framingham, Massachusetts, was known as an excellent marksman, and his owner freed him so he could enlist. Salem fought at Lexington, and at the Battle of Bunker Hill he fired the fatal shot at British Major Pitcairn just as he was rallying his troops. Another Massachusetts black man, Salem Poor, was a hero at the Battle of Bunker Hill.

Yet on July 10, 1775, this trend of integrated fighting was reversed when the American Continental Congress decreed that "no Negroes or vagabonds" could enlist in the newly formed Continental Army. An exception to the law was made in January, 1776, however: Free blacks who had already fought as soldiers could reenlist. Eventually, free blacks, as well as slaves substituting for their masters, were admitted into the army.

In the Continental Navy, hundreds of black sailors also served, with apparently little anxiety from white recruiters. Perhaps it was less controversial because of the long tradition of men of color serving on merchant and whaling ships.

"[TO ACCEPT] ANY ABLE-BODIED SLAVE BETWEEN 18 AND 40 YEARS OF AGE, WHO VOLUNTARILY ENTERS INTO SERVICE . . . WITH THE CONSENT AND AGREEMENT OF HIS MASTER."

→ MARYLAND LAW, OCTOBER 1780

BATTLE OF BUNKER HILL

John Trumbull's famous 1786 oil painting of the Battle of Bunker Hill was once thought to include Peter Salem, a black slave who fought for the American side after he was freed. Recent historians have cast doubt on whether that was really Peter Salem in the picture. Salem is thought to have been the one who fired the shot that killed the British Major Pitcairn.

BLACKS SERVED effectively on both sides as spies. One particularly skillful at this dangerous game was the slave, James, owned by a Virginian named Armistead. With Armistead's permission, James served under General Lafayette. James cleverly sought out a position as servant for the British General Cornwallis. While serving meals to high-ranking officers, James overheard their discussion of military plans. He then secretly sent information about British troop movements back to Lafayette, who then understood Cornwallis' troops' vulnerability as they marched toward the coast. The French fleet could cut them off at sea, while the combined American-French forces could trap them from escaping by land. The subsequent British surrender at Yorktown in 1781 ended the major fighting between the British and the Americans. James Armistead also fed false information to the British, thereby becoming what is known in the espionage business as a "double agent."

After the war, James had trouble securing his freedom, since he had worked for the patriots in secret. But Lafayette personally wrote a letter on his behalf, and the Virginia legislature acted to grant him his freedom. In respectful gratitude, James added the name "Lafayette" to the name of his former master—and henceforth became known as James Armistead Lafayette.

JAMES ARMISTEAD
LAFAYETTE
In 1824, some 40 years after the Revolution, French hero Lafayette returned for a visit. As he rode in his carriage past a crowd of fans at Yorktown, he spotted James and jumped out to embrace him.

GENERAL LAFAYETTE
noted, after the Revolution,
"I would never have drawn my
sword in the cause of America, if
I could have conceived that thereby
I was founding a land of slavery."

WAR *and*

"I NEVER SAW MORE
DISTRESS IN MY LIFE, THAN
WHAT I FOUND AMONG SOME OF THE
POOR **DELUDED** NEGROES
WHICH THE [BRITISH] COULD
NOT TAKE TIME, OR DID NOT
CHUSE TO CARRY OFF WITH
THEM, THEY BEING SICK. . . .
SOME WERE **DYING** AND
MANY CALLING OUT FOR HELP. . . .
MANY OF THEM **TORN** TO
PIECES BY WILD BEASTS. . . ."

❧ CAPTAIN JOHN THORNTON POSEY
AMERICAN LIBERATOR OF GWYNN'S ISLAND, 1776

Chapter 3

ITS AFTERMATH

NOVEMBER 1775

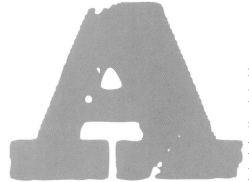 fter the victory at Kemp's Landing, Dunmore's Ethiopians' next battle was at Great Bridge near Norfolk a month later. Half of Dunmore's 600 men belonged to his Ethiopian Regiment. Believing the words of a black spy posing as a loyalist who claimed the patriots had only a few hundred men, Dunmore ordered his troops to cross the bridge. A much larger force suddenly cut them down with gunfire. Many of Dunmore's men were killed, wounded, or captured.

The patriots' victory at the Battle of Great Bridge cut off the only land route to the Tory stronghold of Norfolk. Hundreds of loyalists fled onto Dunmore's already crowded ships.

By New Year's Day, Dunmore's followers were desperate for food and fresh water. Patriots at Norfolk refused the governor's demands to come ashore for supplies. Enraged, Dunmore fired his cannon at the town, setting fire to warehouses along the waterfront. Virginia rebels, bitter over Norfolk's loyalist sympathies, began torching buildings instead of putting out the fire. Within three days, the city was in ashes, with each side blaming the other.

With the destruction of Norfolk, the outlook for Dunmore grew grim. If any of his ships tried to land at their home base, they were easily spotted on the burned-out shoreline. Those on board would have starved if not for the skillful foraging of former slaves.

Then the first signs of the dreaded smallpox appeared in Dunmore's floating city. The illness spread rapidly among people so crowded together, weak from hunger and thirst. They desperately needed a place to land in order to recover and resupply.

ON FEBRUARY 9, 1776, Dunmore's followers finally disembarked near Portsmouth, Virginia. But by then, an epidemic raged. Hardest hit were the former slaves, who had never been inoculated and were now crowded into race-segregated camps.

Dunmore debated whether to have a mass inoculation of his troops. Inoculating meant cutting a healthy person on his hand or arm and inserting the pus of someone who already had the disease. The inoculated person then caught a milder form of the disease. To inoculate thus meant deliberately making his troops sick and vulnerable. Dunmore decided to risk it, but he wanted to move his troops as far away as possible from potential attack. As they boarded their ships to sail into the Chesapeake Bay, they left behind 300 newly dug graves.

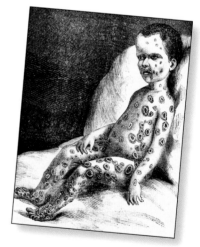

CHILD WITH SMALLPOX
As the disease advanced, pustules appeared on the skin.

They landed at remote Gwynn Island, but runaway slaves arrived daily by small boat. Most immediately caught smallpox. Many were also hit by typhoid

"THE FIRES . . . SPREAD WITH GREAT RAPIDITY, BECAUSE THE . . . PROVINCIAL SOLDIERS . . . SEIZED THE OPPORTUNITY TO PLUNDER AND DESTROY." ❧ H.J. ECKENRODE, HISTORIAN

DESTRUCTION OF
NORFOLK
*With the burning of
Norfolk, Lord Dunmore
and his ship-borne
troops lost their foothold
on land.*

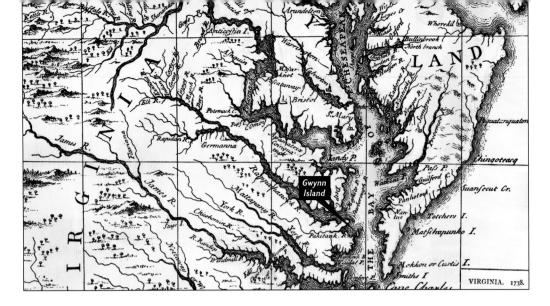

COLONIAL VIRGINIA

This 1732 map of Virginia shows Gwynn Island in the Chesapeake Bay, where Dunmore tried to shelter his troops while they received inoculations against smallpox.

—~~~~~—

fever transmitted by bacteria in food or water. In the days before antibiotics and modern hygiene, typhoid fever was deadly. Meanwhile, the enemy had pursued them and attacked the fleet patrolling near the island. Panicked loyalists began a hasty retreat, leaving their sick comrades behind.

When Virginia patriots stormed the island, they were horrified at what they saw and smelled: about 500 dead bodies, including many women and children. As they had fled, the British had set fire to huts in the contaminated area, not realizing they were burning people alive who were too sick to run.

In retreat, despairing of reinforcement, Dunmore gave up his attempt to hold on to his former colony, Virginia. He burned and ran aground more than half of his ships so they would not fall into enemy hands. Of those remaining, some sailed back to England, while others went to the British fort at St. Augustine, Florida. The pitiful remnant of his Ethiopian Regiment—only about 150 men—set off for British-occupied New York City. Among the group was Henry Washington, one of George Washington's runaway slaves.

One of the original leaders of the Royal Ethiopian Regiment was Titus.

He grew up a slave in a part of New Jersey settled by Quakers. Their church leaders had been among the first colonists to take a stand against slavery. But Titus's Quaker master would not free his slaves, and he whipped them cruelly. Hearing of Dunmore's Proclamation, 22-year-old Titus ran away, traveling down the coast from New Jersey to Virginia to join Lord Dunmore's army.

Surviving the outbreak of disease, Titus returned to his hometown in New Jersey. There he led a group of the area's former slaves known as the Black Brigade in raids to steal provisions. The food they snatched helped feed the thousands of loyalists crowded into British-held New York City. Whenever possible, they liberated slaves during their raids. Although the British did not usually allow nonwhites to be officers, Titus's fellow soldiers respected him so much that many called him Colonel Tye.

In 1780, Colonel Tye was shot in the wrist during an attempt to capture a patriot leader. It was a minor wound, but it became infected, and he died a slow, painful death. His commandos continued their stealth raids under the leadership of Stephen Blucke, formerly a Black Pioneer.

The Black Pioneers were a group of about 70 runaway slaves from the South, mainly from the Carolinas. Unarmed, they did not fight. But their hard labor was vital to the war effort. They constructed the British army's forts, built bridges, cleared roads, and dug trenches.

One of the Black Pioneers' leaders was Thomas Peters. He claimed he was of royal blood from the Yoruba tribe in West Africa. Three times he escaped from slavery, but each time he was caught, whipped, and finally branded. At last he made it over to the British fleet.

The British commander Peters fled to, General Clinton, made a pledge similar to Lord Dunmore's of four years before. From his headquarters in Philipsburg, New York, on June 30, 1779, Clinton offered both a threat and a reward to slaves. Any blacks they captured who'd been fighting on the rebel side, he threatened, would be sold for profit right away. But to those who joined the British, he promised they would be treated as free men and women. This became known as the Philipsburg Proclamation.

Inspired by this offer, as well as by British promises of land to all loyalists after the war, thousands of slaves ran away. Some hid in woods or swamps. But it is estimated that at least 15,000 to 20,000 fled to cities occupied by the British: to Savannah and Charleston and to New York City.

Indirectly and directly, the runaways supported the British war effort. Women worked as nurses, cooks, laundresses, and seamstresses. Men did shoemaking, blacksmithing, carpentry, and other skilled jobs. Some performed the same tasks they had as slaves, but with crucial differences. They chose their occupations and could quit any time, they were paid for their work, and they could not be sold or forcibly separated from their families.

British General Cornwallis's surrender to the Americans at Yorktown on October 19, 1781, marked the end of major combat. Among Cornwallis's troops at Yorktown and nearby Portsmouth, thousands of black loyalists were supporting the British war effort.

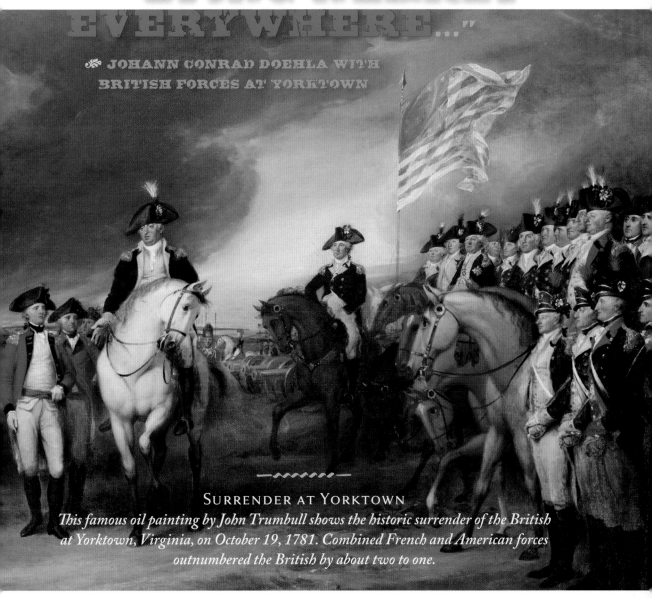

"THE BOMBS. . .
HIT MANY INHABITANTS
AND NEGROES OF THE CITY. . .
ONE SAW MEN
LYING NEARLY
EVERYWHERE..."

— JOHANN CONRAD DOEHLA WITH
BRITISH FORCES AT YORKTOWN

SURRENDER AT YORKTOWN

This famous oil painting by John Trumbull shows the historic surrender of the British at Yorktown, Virginia, on October 19, 1781. Combined French and American forces outnumbered the British by about two to one.

As supplies grew low, the British abandoned these refugees, many of whom died from smallpox, typhus, and hunger. Those who survived were hunted down and forced back into slavery, although Cornwallis was able to rescue several hundred from that fate.

Smallpox
18TH-CENTURY PLAGUE

Few diseases caused more dread and terror than smallpox in the 18th century. Passing from one person to the next, it wiped out entire populations that had not been exposed to it before, such as native American peoples in contact with Europeans for the first time. The smallpox epidemic of 1775-1782 happened at the same time as the American Revolution and killed more Americans than the war with the British did. By the 1700s, people had learned two ways to fight this disease: 1) isolation of those who had it, to keep them away from those who were healthy, and 2) deliberate inoculation with the virus in order to contract a milder version of the illness. Inoculation had already been used in parts of Asia and Africa but was unknown among Europeans. However in 1716, the Puritan minister Cotton Mather wrote friends in London that his African slave had had an inoculation procedure that had given him a mild case of smallpox to protect him from future and more deadly attacks. Mather convinced people to try inoculation in the 1721 outbreak of smallpox in Boston, thereby saving many lives.

As war ended and peace negotiations began, what of the thousands of slaves already freed by the British? At first, Britain agreed to restore all captured property to Americans—and to Americans slaves were property. When word of this agreement leaked out, former slave Boston King recalled, "This dreadful rumour filled us all with inexpressible anguish and terror, especially when we saw our old masters coming from Virginia, North Carolina, and other parts, and seizing upon their slaves in the streets of New York, or even dragging them out of their beds [...]"

But just when the situation began to look grim British commander Sir Guy Carleton presented a new and rather clever argument at the peace talks. The former slaves were not "property" because they had already been freed, he argued, defining as free all those who had reached British lines before November 30,

1782, when the first peace treaty was signed. The American side reluctantly agreed, as long as Britain would eventually pay the owners of the freed slaves.

THIS is to certify to whomsoever it may concern, that the Bearer hereof _Cato Ramsay_ a Negro, reforted to the Britifh Lines, in confequence of the Proclamations of Sir William Howe, and Sir Henry Clinton, late Commanders in Chief in America ; and that the faid Negro has hereby his Excellency Sir Guy Carleton's Permiffion to go to Nova-Scotia, or wherever elfe _She_ may think proper. —

By Order of Brigadier General Birch,

CERTIFICATE OF FREEDOM
This pass allowed its bearer to board one of the ships to Nova Scotia.

— ~~~~~~ —

British Brigadier Samuel Birch was then ordered to determine which of the thousands living in New York City were free. Each person who claimed he'd arrived behind British lines before November 30, 1782—or in the case of small children, if they were born behind the lines by that date—would receive a certificate of freedom allowing him or her to sail away on the British fleet. Their names, ages, descriptions, former masters, and the date they came over to the British were written in "The Book of Negroes." This record was kept in case their masters made claims for compensation. Disputes from either slaves or their owners were heard by a British-American commission.

OUTSIDE OF NEW YORK black loyalists were not as fortunate in securing their freedom at the end of the war. Most British commanders had been careful in their proclamations to state that only slaves of rebels would be free, so former slaves of white loyalists were often out of luck. Furthermore, rebel-owned slaves who did not escape were sometimes captured during raids by the British side and handed over to white loyalists as compensation for property taken away from them by the patriots. So after the war, when thousands of white loyalists were evacuated from the South, many took with them either newly acquired slaves or their old slaves and headed for such British possessions as the Bahamas or the West Indies. Many slaves wound up in Jamaica, where they were forced to do backbreaking work on the sugar plantations.

Nova Scotia

"When [the **POOR** people] had parted with all their **CLOTHES**, even to the blankets, several of them fell down **DEAD** thro' **HUNGER**. Some **KILLED** and ate their dogs and cats and **POVERTY** and distress prevailed on **EVERY** side."

— From Boston King's Memoirs

and FREEDOM

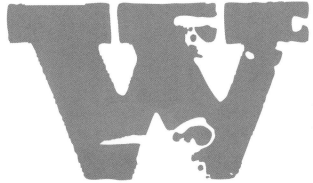

1783

—⁓⁓⁓—

here could the black loyalists go? Few wanted to stay in America, where they greatly feared re-enslavement.

About 400 went to London, where there were few jobs available for them. Many had no option but to crowd into city slums and live on charity. Some would later resettle in Africa.

But Britain was still an imperial power, even though it no longer had its American colonies. The British territory of Nova Scotia, Canada, looked promising: It was nearby, abundant in land, and sparsely populated.

Promised land and provisions, three thousand of the newly freed blacks—along with many more thousands of white loyalists—sailed to Nova Scotia in 1783.

That promise of land was important to the freed slaves. Slavery was legal in Nova Scotia. In fact, many white loyalists took their slaves with them. A black person without land, especially a newcomer without family and friends, would be a second-class citizen and vulnerable to being re-enslaved.

Unfortunately, although there was lots of land, much of it had already

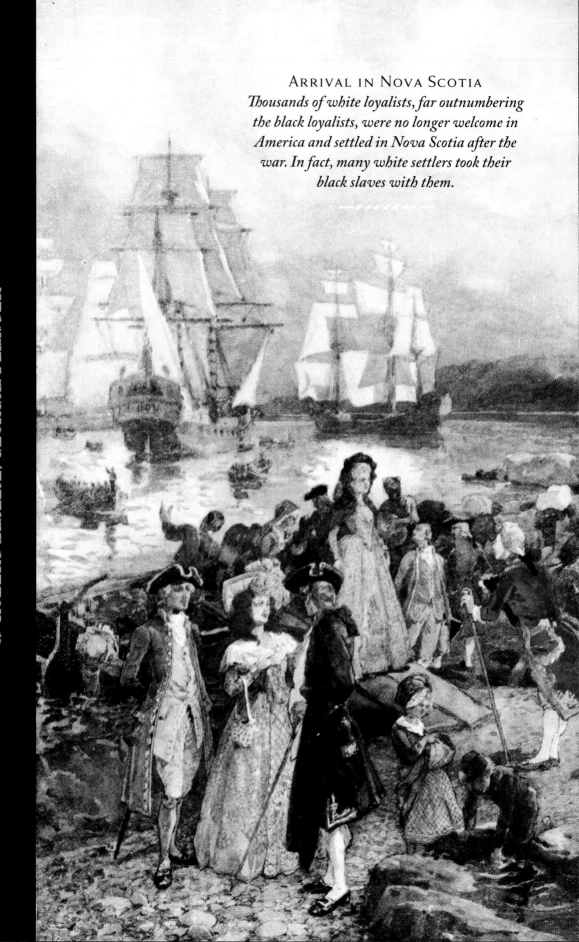

ARRIVAL IN NOVA SCOTIA

Thousands of white loyalists, far outnumbering the black loyalists, were no longer welcome in America and settled in Nova Scotia after the war. In fact, many white settlers took their black slaves with them.

"THIS CURSED WAR HAS RUINED US ALL."

☙ ROBERT BAILLIE, GEORGIA PLANTER

been given to people, including to absentee landlords who had never even settled there. The land left unclaimed was rocky, heavily forested, and infertile. Many black loyalists, without the resources to buy seeds or farming tools, had to become sharecroppers. This meant they worked land owned by others (sometimes white loyalists). Sharecroppers had to give the owner much of the crops they raised. They were poor, hungry, and in debt, and with all their hard labor, they felt as if they were still slaves. Some wound up as indentured servants, binding themselves to a master for a number of years in return for food and shelter.

The black loyalists also felt themselves to be victims of racial discrimination. White loyalists received land sooner, in greater quantities, and in better locations than black loyalists. While waiting for their land, many of the now-free black subjects lived in Birchtown, Nova Scotia (named after General Birch, who had given them their certificates of freedom in New York) but took jobs as day laborers or household servants in the thriving white loyalist town of Shelburne, where they earned far less than whites earned for the same jobs.

WHEN SHELBURNE was first settled, the need for shelter caused a building boom that created jobs for everyone. But after several months of house construction, business slowed down and widespread unemployment, especially among whites, followed. The laid-off white soldiers and workmen rioted in the summer of 1784. The targets of the violence were blacks, whom employers preferred because of their low wages.

Many blacks were beaten, and their homes were destroyed. Only a few prospered—notably Stephen Blucke, Colonel Tye's successor. In Birchtown, he became a teacher in the first school established for black children in North America.

Sergeant Thomas Peters and members of his Black Pioneers unit were on the last ship of loyalists to leave New York. A storm blew their ship off course, and they were stranded in Bermuda over the winter. By the time they finally arrived in Nova Scotia, the Birchtown-Shelburne area was already crowded with loyalists. Peters and his group of black veterans and their families were then sent to another region of Nova Scotia, the Annapolis valley, where they were promised 20 acres each. While still clearing the heavily forested land, they were notified they could not have the land after all, as it was reserved for church use.

Six years after landing in Nova Scotia, Peters and most of the other freed slaves still had not gotten the land they were promised, or only a very small plot of low-quality land. But Peters was not the kind of man to accept unfair treatment quietly. As a former leader of the Black Pioneers army, he was used to acting decisively. After appeals to the governor of Nova Scotia and New Brunswick produced no results, he decided to take his complaint higher and traveled all the way to London. There, he would see his former commander, General Clinton, and the secretary of state and present a petition signed by

LONDON, 1790
Thomas Peters brought a petition to his former commanders.

many of the former slaves. The petition said that they had supported the British during the Revolutionary War because they had been promised freedom and land. Yet they still awaited that land!

His transportation costs paid by small contributions from his many supporters, Peters boarded a ship bound for London. It was a brave move for a freedom-loving man. A black man traveling alone and without funds ran the risk of being captured by an unscrupulous sea captain who might try to sell Peters back into slavery.

When Peters arrived safely in London, a sympathetic Clinton set up meetings for him with high government officials and with the abolitionists, citizens who wanted to abolish slavery.

At about the same time as Peters's visit, a movement was gathering momentum to end slavery in England. Though there were relatively few slaves there, Englishmen profited from selling and buying people, and they owned slaves who worked their plantations in the Caribbean.

One of the abolitionists' ideas was to resettle former slaves in Sierra Leone, West Africa. A group including several hundred of London's black loyalists had moved there in 1787. Arriving during the rainy season, they'd had no time to plant crops. Many had become ill and died. The town they had established was destroyed by a neighboring African tribe, the Temne.

But to the British government, bankers, and abolitionists, moving the freed slaves from Nova Scotia to Sierra Leone still seemed like a win-win proposition. The British would be able to populate their far-off colony and provide the land promised the black loyalists. Moreover, they would earn money by trading in such highly valued commodities as rice, cotton, coffee, and sugar to replace the immoral but still profitable slave trade.

Thomas Peters, too, decided Sierra Leone was the place to realize his dream of becoming a free, independent land-owner. But he could not do it alone. He would have to convince many others. To help "sell" the plan, Peters returned to Nova Scotia with Lieutenant John Clarkson. Brother of a well-known abolitionist, Clarkson of the British Royal Navy traveled with Peters throughout Nova Scotia and tried to persuade ex-slaves to move to West Africa.

Every free black of proven "good character" was promised free passage to Sierra Leone. Once there, he would receive land—20 acres of land for himself, 10 for his wife, and 5 for each of his children.

Clarkson promised this land would not be taxed. But he made his promise without the knowledge or approval of the Sierra Leone Company, the company that would finance and manage the settlement, and it would later come back to haunt him.

One spur to recruitment, in addition to the lure of free and untaxed land, was just how bad conditions had become in Nova Scotia. The year 1789 brought severely cold weather and famine to Canada. It was so bad in Nova Scotia that the province became jokingly known as Nova Scarcity. One of the black loyalists, Boston King, described conditions like this:

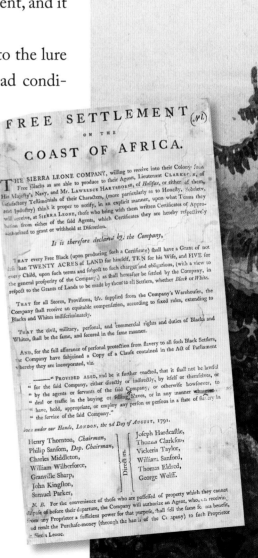

—————

THE LURE OF A BETTER PLACE

The Sierra Leone Company advertised free passage and land for black Nova Scotians willing to relocate to West Africa (near right).

Many of the black settlers had arrived in Nova Scotia with few possessions and little protection from the cold climate (far right).

"MANY OF THE POOR PEOPLE WERE COMPELLED TO SELL THEIR BEST GOWNS FOR FIVE POUNDS OF FLOUR IN ORDER TO SUPPORT LIFE."

FROM BOSTON KING'S MEMOIRS

The British ABOLITIONISTS

Granville Sharpe, John Clarkson's more famous brother Thomas Clarkson, and British Parliament member William Wilberforce were part of a small group of white, upper-class Englishmen who believed that slavery was cruel and inhumane. They worked tirelessly for many years to get the practice banned not only in England, but also throughout the British Empire, and to end the lucrative slave trade dominated by British seamen and merchants. Originally laughed at as impractical dreamers, the abolitionists gained popular support through such means as publishing the memoirs of a former slave named Equiano, who described the cruelty of slavery; organizing a boycott of sugar (sugar was grown on West Indies plantations using slave labor); and distributing posters with drawings of slave ships showing how many slaves were crammed into one hold. The abolitionists played a key role in helping the black loyalists resettle in Sierra Leone.

"Many of the poor people were compelled to sell their best gowns for five pounds of flour, in order to support life. When they had parted with all their clothes, even to their blankets, several of them fell down dead in the streets, thro' hunger. Some killed and eat their dogs and cats; and poverty and distress prevailed on every side; so that to my great grief I was obliged to leave Birchtown, because I could get no employment. I traveled from place to place, to procure the necessaries of life, but in vain."

Thousands of white loyalists returned to the United States. But this was not an option for black loyalists, who feared recapture and enslavement. Sierra Leone, with its year-round warm climate and fertile soil, sounded better than Nova Scotia.

Another condition that helped recruitment was the religious revival sweeping Nova Scotia. Black loyalists no longer had to hide group religious practices from masters forbidding mass meetings of slaves. Former slave-turned-preacher David George wrote of one of his first nights in Nova Scotia: "I began to sing the first night, in the woods at a camp, for there were no houses built. . . . the Black people came from far and near, and it was so new to them: I kept on so every night in the week and appointed a meeting for the first Lord's day in a valley between two hills, close by the river; and a great number of White and Black people came, and I was so overjoyed with having an opportunity once more of preaching the word of God that after I had given out the hymn, I could not speak for tears."

Exulting in their new freedom, they established Methodist, Baptist, and Anglican congregations, each led by a charismatic preacher. Clarkson and Peters visited these churches to plead their case. When minister Boston King and his wife Violet decided to go to Sierra Leone, their entire congregation was inspired to go with them. The same thing happened with the blind, lame preacher Moses Wilkinson and his Methodist church; David George with the Baptists; and John Marrant with the Huntingdonians (a Methodist sect named after their founder, the Countess of Huntingdon).

THERE WAS strong opposition to the plan. The government of Nova Scotia did not want to see its population shrink, and white employers didn't want to lose low-wage workers. Employers also worried that only the weakest, least employable blacks would be left behind. It was ruled that any person in debt or even working as an indentured servant would not be allowed to leave until they paid off their debts.

Even so, about 1,200 black loyalists, nearly one-half of the black settlers—including over 400 young people age 16 and under—sailed from Halifax in January, 1792. They were bound for the land of their ancestors—Africa.

AFRICA: *The*

"THE PROMISES MADE US
BY YOUR AGENTS IN NOVA SCOTIA
WERE VERY **GOOD** AND FAR
BETTER THAN WE EVER
HAD BEFORE FROM **WHITE**
PEOPLE AND NO MAN CAN HELP
SAYING MR. CLARKSON BEHAVED
AS KIND AND **TENDER**
TO US AS IF HE WAS
OUR **FATHER. . . ."**

CATO PERKINS, ISAAC ANDERSON, ET AL.
IN THEIR PETITION PRESENTED TO
SIERRA LEONE COMPANY IN LONDON, 1793

Chapter 5

PROMISED LAND

MARCH 1792

hose who boarded the ships bound for Africa carried tools to work the land; pumpkins, squash, watermelon, and cabbage seeds; Bibles and hymn books; and guns for protection. All traveled with high hopes that their long-delayed dream of owning their own land would soon be realized. Leading the expedition was their recruiter, Lieutenant Clarkson.

Many of the emigrants were already weak and sickly from their lives of poverty in Nova Scotia. The winter weather unleashed storm after storm; the seas were rough; and food rations dwindled. Sixty-five of the travelers died before they reached the shores of Africa. Even Lieutenant Clarkson caught fever and was thought to be dead. He was wrapped in a shroud and was about to be thrown overboard when someone saw him move.

Still, the majority survived the trip, including the 104-year-old mother of Cato Perkins, the new pastor of the Huntingdonian Methodist group. She had come with the desire to be buried in her native Sierra Leone.

Upon first landing in March 1792, Sierra Leone looked like paradise compared to Nova Scotia. The sun shone down and warmed them. Green forests spilled down the hillsides to pristine white sand beaches. The waters swarmed with colorful fish. Joyfully singing hymns, the Nova Scotians (as they came to be known) broke ground for a city they proudly named Freetown.

BUT SOON they encountered the ugly side of life in the tropics: torrential rain storms that washed away the seeds they planted, tornadoes, hurricanes, swarms of insects, poisonous snakes, wild animals, and more deadly diseases—this time, malaria and yellow fever.

Clarkson had requested that the Sierra Leone Company directors who had already arrived have the land plots surveyed, cleared, and ready for distribution, and to have temporary housing and food prepared as well. However, when they arrived, nothing had been done. To protect themselves from the rainy season, the settlers made tents out of their ships' sails. They ate the salted fish and worm-infested bread left over from their voyage, but still another 40 became ill and died.

They also had problems with their neighbors. Not many miles downriver were the slave traders of Bance Island. The island was infamous as the fort where captured West Africans were held crowded together in chains before being shipped across the Atlantic to become slaves in South Carolina. Imagine the horror of the former slaves when they saw ships loaded up with newly enslaved people sailing right past Freetown!

Their other problem neighbors were the native Temne tribe. Their chief believed he had merely loaned them the use of his land, whereas the settlers thought the Sierra Leone Company had bought the land for good.

Lieutenant John Clarkson had assumed his leadership duties would end when they landed in Sierra Leone and he could return to his home in England. He was still weak from fever, and his fiancée awaited his return. But he soon learned that the Sierra Leone Company expected him to stay on to govern the settlement.

A New Home

A Portuguese explorer named the country Sierra Leone or "Lion Mountains." It is unclear if he meant that the coastal region with its many mountains looked like lion's teeth, or if he thought the thunderstorms coming in over the mountains sounded like a lion's roar.

BANCE ISLAND

Bance Island was the large British slave castle about 20 miles upriver from Freetown, Sierra Leone. This is where captured Africans were held in chains while awaiting the arrival of slave ships to carry them across the Atlantic to the Americas.

Sergeant Thomas Peters was also surprised by Clarkson's appointment as governor. As co-recruiter with Clarkson in Nova Scotia, Peters had assumed he would be the leader of the new settlement. But the all-white Sierra Leone Company Council gave him no role. Remembering the abolitionists' promise of a self-governing, democratic black colony, Peters grew bitter.

Clarkson, too, would discover he had limited authority. His every move, including the surveying of land, had to be approved by the company's slow-moving council. Clarkson and Peters soon became rivals. The former slaves felt more comfortable telling their problems to their old leader, Peters, rather than to Clarkson, especially after learning that Clarkson had met with the neighboring slave traders. They also feared that Clarkson, like the white rulers in Nova Scotia, would be slow to deliver on their promised land. The

Clarkson-Peters quarrel escalated when Clarkson heard of a plot to have him overthrown, with Peters as his replacement. Clarkson angrily called an emergency meeting of the black settlers under a giant cotton tree. There he publicly called Peters a traitor and threatened to hang him from that very tree.

A short time later, Peters was accused—and found guilty by a jury of his peers—of stealing from a dead man (Peters claimed the man owed him money). Days later, Peters contracted malaria and died, just four months after landing in Sierra Leone.

Yet many of the settlers still loved Clarkson. They viewed him as a Moses who had led them to their "Promised Land." They were sad when Clarkson tearfully announced in December 1792 that he was returning to England. His health was still poor, he said, and the company directors back in London wished to meet with him. His fiancée was growing impatient. But it was only a temporary leave, he said. He promised to return.

Surveying the land—a necessary step before it could be divided and parceled out to the settlers—moved at a snail's pace, slowed by the constant rain. The soil was thin, the land was covered by steep hills and heavy forests, and land near the waterways was reserved for Sierra Leone Company councilmen. Many settlers were forced to work menial jobs for the company for low wages that bought them little at the company-owned store (the only place to buy goods). Pastor Cato Perkins and his friend Isaac Anderson decided to follow the activist example of Thomas Peters. They would travel to

—〰〰〰—

SHACKLES OF SLAVERY
Shackles used to bind slaves' legs came in all sizes, as children were captured as well as adults. Any children born to slaves in captivity became the property of the master as well.

53

London to complain to the Sierra Leone Company's board of directors.

Like Peters, they wrote out a petition. It said, "The Promises made us by your Agents in Nova Scotia were very good and far better than we ever had before from White People." But, it continued, "the Rains is now set in and the Lands is not all given out yet so we have no time to clear any for this year to come." They pleaded that though "we have not had the Education which White Men have yet we have feeling the same as other Human Beings and would wish to do every thing we can for to make our Children free and happy after us. . . ."

But the company's board of directors did not listen. They had fired Clarkson and would not let him go back to Africa, or even meet with Perkins and Anderson in London. Disappointed, the two men returned to Sierra Leone. The next governors would be far less sympathetic. Feelings of betrayal and injustice rose.

—✦✦✦✦✦—

FREETOWN
The town of Freetown was built on the site of the original Granville Town settled in the late 1780s by a group of black loyalists from London. Many in Granville either deserted or died from disease, and the town itself was burned to the ground by the neighboring Temne people.

"I DO NOT KNOW OF ANY EMPLOYMENT IN THE WORLD THAT WOULD BE MORE PLEASING. . . THAN MY BEST ATTEMPT TO ESTABLISH THIS COLONY."

JOHN CLARKSON

IRONICALLY, one of the issues that brought matters near the breaking point was taxation. Many Nova Scotians had fought on the British side when their American masters had objected to the same thing—taxation without representation. Clarkson had promised their land would not be taxed. But after Clarkson was fired, the company directors felt they had a freer hand.

With an urgent need for revenue to rebuild Freetown after it was attacked by French warships during the war between France and Britain in 1796, company officials sent instructions to collect an annual tax of one shilling per acre. Thinking it a small fee, the company underestimated the fierce opposition it would raise. The freed slaves felt that once again a promise made to them by the white man was being broken. They believed a tax on their land was a threat to their independence. If they could not pay it, they could be evicted and re-enslaved like the people on Bance Island.

Meanwhile, the settlement prospered. Black settlers no longer died from

Settling in WEST AFRICA

Portuguese navigators named the land Serra Lyoa (Lion Mountains), and European traders made the coastal land a regular stop on their voyages, where they picked up ivory, timber, and slaves. Bance Island became their place to hold slaves bound for the Americas. But this is also the place where English abolitionists such as Granville Sharp had the idea of settling freed slaves in their original African homeland. It would not only give them a land of their own but also solve the problem of the homeless poor living on charity in London. Over 400 passengers (including many of the black loyalists who had settled in London as well as their white wives) left England for Sierra Leone in 1787 to establish Granville Town in a province they proudly named Freedom (near the present-day Freetown). While some had volunteered to resettle, others were beggars forced by the government onto the ships. Many died from disease in the first year, and their town was destroyed during an attack by the Temne tribe. In 1792, the Nova Scotian black loyalists fared better. Inspired by such attempts, freed American slaves began organizing settlement of neighboring Liberia in 1822.

disease or starvation. They successfully grew edible crops such as yams, beans, and cassava. The women in Freetown prospered as they became traders, shopkeepers, teachers, and even preachers. One former slave began harvesting coffee, producing the region's first cash crop. A police force was created to maintain order, and a militia was formed to defend the colony against outside attacks. There were trials by jury, and at least half the jury had to be the same race as the defendant. Residents began electing their own representatives to advise the Sierra Leone Company. Free public schools were established and churches flourished.

But after Clarkson left, distrust and animosity increased between the settlers, ever-vigilant about safeguarding their rights, and the Sierra Leone Company and its subsequent governors. In 1800, some of the more politicized settlers banded together, drew up their own laws, and announced that the governor and his Company council could only govern in matters related to Company business. The governor declared them in rebellion. The British secretly landed a ship at Freetown. On this ship were not only British soldiers, but hundreds of former slaves from Jamaica (known as "maroons") being brought in to further populate the colony. Promised their own land and eager to show their loyalty, the maroons attacked the rebels and captured them. Two rebel leaders were hanged.

Finally, in 1808, the British government took over. As a crown colony, Sierra Leone played a key role in the campaign to stop the slave trade, which the British banned in 1808. The British Navy patrolled the waters off West Africa looking for illegal slave ships. When they captured one, they freed the slaves and sent them ashore to Sierra Leone. Soon the original settlers were outnumbered by the newly freed slaves, as well as by thousands of maroons from Jamaica. Still, the settlers from Nova Scotia kept themselves separate from the rest of the population, proud of their long tradition of political independence. Their descendents live in Freetown.

EPILOGUE

It is often said that history is written by the winners. Americans won their rebellion against British rule—and are proud of recalling the struggle to become an independent nation. But what of the thousands of people who were brutally dragged from their homes and families in Africa to America? To the slaves, the Patriots' cries to live free from British tyranny must have rung hollow indeed. They, too, wanted to live free.

But freedom does not come easily. Often it must be gained through a long, hard struggle against the institutions and people that enslave. Joining the British forces during a time of war was a calculated risk requiring courage as well as cunning. Runaway slaves faced the possibility of recapture and severe punishment, even death. Even if they succeeded in eluding their masters, they faced an uncertain future and the strong possibility of death, either in battle or by disease, or reenslavement in an even harsher environment.

They took that risk because a promise was made to them: If they supported the British, they could earn freedom and land. Owning land, in those days, was a critical element in ensuring their continued independence. They trusted they would receive fair treatment under British law.

Many of the runaways radically transformed themselves once they became free. Some, such as Thomas Peters, Isaac Anderson, and Colonel Tye, showed courage and strength by serving in the British armed forces. Others such as David George, Boston King, and Moses Wilkinson, for the first time were free to preach what they believed and took on the role of religious leaders. Still others passed through harrowing ordeals to go on to lead productive lives as free men and women.

Even after escaping the institutional constraints of a system that had forced them to be slaves, living as free men and women was not easy. Like so many settlers throughout history, they faced the unknown and the challenges of creating a new colony out of wilderness. In Nova Scotia, they found a harsh and unwelcoming environment. In Sierra Leone, that vision of paradise they glimpsed when they first arrived turned out to be a mirage. Behind the dazzling natural beauty they found cruel and deadly obstacles, from tropical storms, wild animals, hostile local people, and disease, to unfair treatment by the directors of the Sierra Leone Company. In addition, they faced the ever-present reminder of slavery in the form of slave traders living just a few miles away.

Many died. But many survived, even prospered. Their settlement became a haven, a place where black loyalists and freed slaves could live peacefully. In their years in West Africa, the black loyalists enjoyed some amount of self-government. Many eventually received their promised land, although it was frequently not of the quality or quantity they'd expected. Others settled in Freetown, where women as well as men worked as teachers, shopkeepers, or traders.

As free men and women, they enjoyed the right to trial by a jury of peers, and elected representatives. If they believed an injustice had been committed, they could petition the governing officials.

The black loyalists proved they could live and thrive as free men and women. That seems unsurprising now, but it was a radical, empowering example back then. The settlers understood and exercised their rights and duties as free subjects of the British Empire—and they passionately tried to defend these rights. They were able to live free.

TIMELINE

June 22, 1772—Somerset Decision: Judge Mansfield rules that the law of England does not permit a slave to be forcibly removed from England against his will.

April 21, 1775—Lord Dunmore orders Royal Marines to sneak gunpowder out of Williamsburg's powder house and to transfer it to his warship.

April 23, 1775—Lord Dunmore threatens to "declare Freedom to the Slaves and reduce the City of Williamsburg to Ashes" if attacked.

April 28, 1775—News reaches Williamsburg of battles at Lexington and Concord nine days earlier.

June 8, 1775—Lord Dunmore and his family flee Williamsburg.

Early July 1775—Lord Dunmore moves his warship and several ships of Loyalists including former slaves to Hampton Roads near Chesapeake Bay.

October 8, 1775—General George Washington and his generals unanimously agree to exclude all slaves from army; the majority say to exclude all blacks from military service.

November 14, 1775—Dunmore's army of freed slaves helps win the Battle of Kemp's Landing.

November 14, 1775—Lord Dunmore prints and distributes his proclamation to free the rebels' slaves who fight for the king.

December 9, 1775—Patriot militias triumph over the combined Loyalist/British/Royal Ethiopian Regiment at the Battle of Great Bridge, forcing them back to their ships.

January 1-3, 1776—Norfolk, a Loyalist stronghold, is destroyed.

Early June 1776—Lord Dunmore establishes a camp on Gwynn Island while attempting mass inoculation against a smallpox epidemic raging among former slaves.

July 9, 1776—Lord Dunmore evacuates troops from Gwynn Island, leaving hundreds of the former slaves dead of smallpox and typhoid.

August 6, 1776—Lord Dunmore, along with his regular soldiers and the remains of his Royal Ethiopian Regiment, sails up to New York City.

January 1778—George Washington approves the First Rhode Island Regiment, an entire regiment of black soldiers in Rhode Island.

Winter 1779—Colonel Tye's Black Brigade joins with Queen's Rangers to carry out guerrilla warfare around New York and New Jersey.

June 30, 1779—Sir Henry Clinton issues the Philipsburg Proclamation, offering to free any rebel slave who can escape to British protection.

September 1780—Colonel Tye receives a minor wound during a raid. It becomes infected, and he dies.

October 1780—The all-black unit 2nd Company, 4th Connecticut Regiment is formed.

October 19, 1782—The British surrender at Yorktown, including thousands of black troops on both sides.

November 29, 1782—The Treaty of Paris is signed to end the Revolutionary War.

April 28–November 23, 1783—Thousands of freed black loyalists are evacuated to British ports in England and Nova Scotia. White loyalists and their slaves are evacuated in even greater numbers.

May 4, 1783—Over 3,000 black men, women, and children on 30 transport ships arrive at Port Roseway, Nova Scotia, from New York.

July 1784—An anti-black race riot is held in Nova Scotia.

Early 1786—Henry Smeathman's proposal to resettle London poor in Sierra Leone is studied.

February 1787—411 black (plus about 60 white) colonists leave England for Sierra Leone, West Africa.

1789—Famine and a severe winter hits Nova Scotia.

November 1789—Tribal King Jimmy attacks and burns Granville Town in Sierra Leone.

October 1790—Sergeant Thomas Peters arrives in London with a petition of complaint from over 200 black loyalist families.

October 1791–January 1792—Thomas Peters and John Clarkson travel in Nova Scotia trying to recruit settlers for Sierra Leone.

January 16, 1792—1196 settlers from New Brunswick/Nova Scotia set out for Sierra Leone aboard 15 ships.

March 1792—Nova Scotians' ships arrive in Sierra Leone.

June 25, 1792—Thomas Peters dies of malaria in Sierra Leone.

December 29, 1792—John Clarkson sails back to London.

October 1793—Cato Perkins and Isaac Anderson go to London to present a petition of complaint to top officials of the Sierra Leone Company.

September 1794—A French fleet attacks Freetown, Sierra Leone, and almost destroys it.

May 20, 1800—Governor Ludlam rejects the black settlers' judicial appointments.

September 1800—A group of Sierra Leone settlers draws up their own set of laws, which is called an act of mutiny.

October 1800—Newly arrived maroons attack the Sierra Leone rebels.

December 22, 1800—Isaac Anderson and Frank Patrick are tried and hung for treason.

March 1807—President Thomas Jefferson signs a law banning the importation of slaves into the United States.

May 1, 1807—The British slave trade is officially banned.

January 1, 1808—The British officially make Sierra Leone a Crown Colony.

RESOURCE GUIDE

BOOKS FOR YOUNG READERS

(NOTE: The following nonfiction focuses on African-American involvement on the patriot side only)

Brennan, Linda Crotta; and Cheryl Kirk Noll. *The Black Regiment of the American Revolution.* Moon Mountain Publishing, 2004.

Cox, Clinton. *Come All ye Brave Soldiers: Blacks in the Revolutionary War.* Scholastic Press, 1999.

Davis, Burke. *Black Heroes of the American Revolution.* Orlando: Harcourt Press, 1976.

Haskins, Jim; Clinton Cox, and Brenda Wilkinson. *Black Stars of Colonial Times and the Revolutionary War: African Americans Who Lived Their Dreams.* Jossey-Bass, 2002.

Reef, Catherine. *African Americans in the Military.* New York: Facts on File, 2004. Individual profiles of famous African Americans throughout history who have served in the military, from Crispus Attucks to Colin Powell.

(fiction)
Elliott, L.M. *Give Me Liberty.* New York: Harper Collins, 2006. Laced with real events and leaders, *Give Me Liberty* explores the American Revolution through the eyes of a 13-year-old indentured servant, an eccentric schoolmaster, a hotheaded apprentice, and a runaway slave in Williamsburg, Virginia, who runs away to join the British Royal Ethiopian Regiment.

Figley, Marty Rhodes. *Prisoner for Liberty.* Minneapolis: Millbrook/Lerner Publishing Company, 2008. This entry in the On My Own History series celebrates the heroism of an African-American teen in the Revolutionary War. Born free, 15-year-old James Forten joined the crew of the *Royal Louis* as a sailor. When the British captured the ship, he refused the chance to escape to help a sickly white friend.

BOOKS FOR OLDER READERS

Hill, Lawrence. *Someone Knows My Name: A Novel.* W.W. Norton: 2007.

Johnson, Charles; Smith, Patricia. *Africans in America: America's Journey through Slavery.* New York: Harcourt for WGBH Educational Foundation, 1998.

Pybus, Cassandra. *Epic Journeys of Freedom.* Boston: Beacon Press, 2006.

Quarles, Benjamin. *Negro in the American Revolution.* Chapel Hill, NC: University of North Carolina Press, 1961.

Schama, Simon. *Rough Crossings.* New York: HarperCollins, 2006.

PLACES TO VISIT

You can see the gunpowder house, the Governor's Palace, and occasional reenactments of the Royal Ethiopian Regiment and patriots at Colonial Williamsburg, Virginia.

WEB SITES

Colonial Williamsburg: http://www.history.org

For more about the loyalists in Nova Scotia, see the Black Loyalist Heritage Society website at www.blackloyalist.com

The On-line Institute for Advanced Loyalist Studies: www.royalprovincial.com

Government of Nova Scotia: http://museum.gov.ns.ca/blackloyalists/struggle.htm

INDEX

SOURCES

CHAPTER 1: *Liberty to Slaves*

Page 8: "And I do hereby declare. . ." is from Dunmore's Proclamation issued on November 7, 1775, from onboard his ship.

Page 11: "By the living God...lay the town in ashes!" as quoted in "Lord Dunmore Emerges from the Shadows" by Mark Ogden, *Daughters of the American Revolution Magazine* 116(5), 1982, pp. 366-369.

Accounts of the Williamsburg powder house incident can be found in *The Day the American Revolution Began: April 19, 1775* by William H. Hallahan. New York: Perennial, 2001; and *A Son of Thunder: Patrick Henry and the American Republic* by Henry Mayer. New York: Grove Press, 1991.

For descriptions of life on Dunmore's crowded ships, I was aided by *The Governor's Island* by Peter Jennings Wrike. Gwynn, Virginia: The Gwynn's Island Museum, 1993.

I gained insights about the slaves who fled to the British from discussions with and lectures by Harvey Bakari, Colonial Williamsburg's manager of African American History Interpretation; Sylvia Frey, professor emeritus at Tulane University's history department, New Orleans, and author of *Water from the Rock: Black Resistance in a Revolutionary Age,* Princeton: Princeton University Press, 1991; and Simon Schama, historian and professor at Columbia University, author of *Rough Crossings: Britain, The Slaves and the American Revolution,* New York: HarperCollins Books, 2006.

At the Library of Congress, I read microfilm of *The Virginia Gazette* from November 1775 to learn about the reaction to Lord Dunmore's proclamation. I also read many advertisements for runaway slaves, some referencing Dunmore.

I enjoyed several visits to Colonial Williamsburg, during which I looked at the powder house, toured the Governor's Palace, and went to a Black History weekend during which I saw men reenact runaway slave trials.

Page 14: "If a governor can . . . give freedom. . ." is from "Reminiscences of the American Revolution" in *The Military and Naval Magazine* 5(5), July 1835, p. 326.

CHAPTER 2: *And Some Joined the Patriots*

Page 20: "Why stand we here idle?" is from Patrick Henry's speech, delivered to the Virginia convention of delegates meeting at Henrico Parish Church in Richmond on March 20, 1775.

Page 22: "Neither the hue of their complexion. . ." is quoted in *An Imperfect God, George Washington, His Slaves, and the Creation of America* by Henry Wiencek. New York: Farrar, Straus and Giroux, 2003, p. 215.

Page 23: Estimates of how many slaves escaped to British protection vary widely. Schama, *Rough Crossings,* p. 132. Schama also notes on p. 8 that Thomas Jefferson wrote that as many as 30,000 slaves escaped Virginia alone.

Page 25: "[To accept] any able-bodied slave. . ." is taken from "The Revolution's Black Soldiers" by Robert A. Selig. www.americanrevolution.org includes Selig's article and others, as well as primary documents.

Page 27: "I would never have drawn my sword. . ." appears in Wiencek, p. 261.

CHAPTER 3: *War and Its Aftermath*

Page 28: "I never saw more distress. . ." as quoted in Schama, p. 87.

To learn about smallpox, I read *Pox Americana: The Great Smallpox Epidemic of 1775-82* by Elizabeth A. Fenn. New York: Hill & Wang, 2001.

Page 31: "The fires . . . spread with great rapidity. . ." as quoted in *The Revolution in Virginia* by H.J. Eckenrode. Boston: Houghton Mifflin, 1916, p. 86.

Page 35: "The bombs. . . hit . ." as quoted in *Africans in America: America's Journey Through Slavery* by Charles Johnson, Patricia Smith, and the WGBH Series Research Team. New York: Harcourt, 1998, p. 191.

Page 36: "This dreadful rumour. . ." is from the "Memoirs of the Life of Boston King" published in the *Methodist Magazine,* April 1798. Available in the Rare Books Division at the Library of Congress.

CHAPTER 4: *Nova Scotia and Freedom*

Page 38: "When [the poor people] had parted. . ." appears in Boston King's memoirs.

Page 40: "This cursed war. . ." is cited in Johnson et al., p. 198.

Page 45: "Many of the poor people were compelled. . ." is from Boston King's memoirs.

Among the books I found helpful was a compilation of articles in *Loyalists in Nova Scotia,* edited by Donald Wetmore and Lester B. Sellick. Hantsport, Nova Scotia: Lancelot Press, 1983.

CHAPTER 5: *The Promised Land*

Page 46: "I began to sing the first night. . ." is from memoirs David George wrote for the *Annual Baptist Registry* (1793), p. 473.

Pages 48 and 54: "The promises made us..." are from petitions from the settlers in Sierra Leone, collected and edited by Christopher Fyfe in *Our Children Free and Happy: Letters from Black Settlers in Africa in the 1790s.* Edinburgh, 1991.

Page 55: "I do not know of any employment. . ." as quoted in Schama, p. 358.

There are several books for adults that cover in great detail the migration to Nova Scotia and Sierra Leone. Among them are: Clifford, Mary Louise. *From Slavery to Freetown, Black Loyalists After the American Revolution.* North Carolina: McFarland & Company, 1999; and Walker, James W. St. G. *The Black Loyalists Search for a Promised Land in Nova Scotia and Sierra Leone, 1783-1870.* University of Toronto Press, 1992.

Some of the primary sources I read included Governor John Clarkson's *Diary and the Origins of Sierra Leone,* which I found extracts of in the *Journal of African Studies* 5(1), Spring 1978, at the library of the Smithsonian's Museum of African Art. Also in *Sierra Leone Studies,* 1925.

This book is dedicated to Roosevelt LeVert Prince and to his entire family whom I have been privileged to have as my dear neighbors.

Special thanks to Harvey Bakari, Colonial Williamsburg's manager of African American History Interpretation, who has made this story come alive for me; my wonderful editor at National Geographic, Jennifer Emmett, who gently spurs me on to greater efforts, as well as the enthusiastic and capable Sue Macy and Marfe Ferguson Delano; Sylvia R. Frey, a great and early scholar in this field, who was so generous with her time when I was in New Orleans; Simon Schama, the British historian who wrote a wonderful book and documentary on the subject, and who encouraged me to write it for children, too; Tom Mann, my favorite sleuth, for his enthusiastic research assistance at Library of Congress; Matthew Whitman Blair, who took a red pen to certain sections of his mother's purple prose and did a few spots of research as well; and a final thanks to my beloved mother, Frances P. Whitman, who always believed in the importance of this story. Thanks to David, too, for loving support, and my better half, Bob, who is my second pair of eyes as well as sounding board for all my writing endeavors.

The National Geographic Society is one of the world's largest nonprofit scientific and educational organizations. Founded in 1888 to "increase and diffuse geographic knowledge," the Society works to inspire people to care about the planet. It reaches more than 325 million people worldwide each month through its official journal, *National Geographic*, and other magazines; National Geographic Channel; television documentaries; music; radio; films; books; DVDs; maps; exhibitions; school publishing programs; interactive media; and merchandise. National Geographic has funded more than 9,000 scientific research, conservation and exploration projects and supports an education program combating geographic illiteracy. For more information, visit nationalgeographic.com.

For more information, please call 1-800-NGS LINE (647-5463) or write to the following address:
National Geographic Society
1145 17th Street N.W.
Washington, D.C. 20036-4688 U.S.A.
Visit us online at www.nationalgeographic.com/books
For librarians and teachers: www.ngchildrensbooks.org
More for kids from National Geographic:
kids.nationalgeographic.com
For information about special discounts for bulk purchases,
please contact National Geographic Books Special Sales: ngspecsales@ngs.org
For rights or permissions inquiries, please contact National
Geographic Books Subsidiary Rights: ngbookrights@ngs.org

Library of Congress Cataloging-in-Publication Data
Blair, Margaret Whitman.
  Liberty or death : the surprising story of runaway slaves who sided with the British during the American Revolution / by Margaret Blair.
     p. cm.
  Includes bibliographical references and index.
  ISBN 978-1-4263-0590-0 (hardcover : alk. paper) — ISBN 978-1-4263-0591-7 (library binding : alk. paper)
  1. United States—History—Revolution, 1775-1783—Participation, African American—Juvenile literature. 2. United States—History—Revolution, 1775-1783—African Americans—Juvenile literature. 3. United States—History—Revolution, 1775-1783—British forces—Juvenile literature. 4. African Americans—History—18th century—Juvenile literature. 5. African American soldiers—History—18th century—Juvenile literature. 6. African American loyalists—History—Juvenile literature. 7. Fugitive slaves—United States—History—18th century—Juvenile literature. 8. Freedmen—United States—History—18th century—Juvenile literature. 9. Slaves—Emancipation—United States—History—18th century—Juvenile literature. 10. Slavery—United States—History—18th century—Juvenile literature. I. Title.
  E269.N3B55 2010
  973.3'46—dc22   2009026853

Printed in China
09/TS/1

Design by James Hiscott, Jr.
Illustrations research by Annette Kiesow

Cover: © Illustration by Kurt Miller; 4-5: © The Art Archive/ Musée des Arts Africains et Océaniens/ Gianni Dagli Orti; 7, 12, 24-25, 26, 27, 31: © The Granger Collection. New York; 9, 21, 29 (both): © Shutterstock; 11: © Virginia Historical Society; 13: © The Library of Congress; 14, 42: © Tate, London Art Resource, NY; 17: © The National Archives, UK; 19: © Vernon Wooten/ Colonial Williamsburg Foundation; 22: © Anne S. K. Brown Military Collection, Brown University Library; 30: © Mary Evans Picture Library; 32: © North Wind Picture Archives; 34-35: © Yale University Art Library/ Art Resource, NY; 37, 44 (inset): © Nova Scotia Archives and Records Management; 39, 49: © Stockbyte/ Getty Images; 40: © Landing of the Loyalists in 1783 by Paul Sandham/ Private Collection/ The Bridgeman Art Library; 45: © Watercolour by Robert Petley/ Library and Archives Canada; 51: © A View of the New Settlement in the River at Sierra Leona on the Coast of Guinea in Africa, English School/ British Library, London, UK/ The Bridgeman Art Library; 52: © Bance Island, River Sierra Leone, Coast of Africa, Perspective Point at 1, c.1805 by Corry/ Private Collection/ Michael Graham-Stewart/ The Bridgeman Art Library; 53: © A set of anklets, 19th century (iron)/ Private Collection/ Michael Graham-Stewart/ The Bridgeman Art Library; 54-55; © Bettmann/ Corbis.